Graphic Organizer Ac[...]
with Answer Key

MW00825140

HOLT

Civics

HOLT, RINEHART AND WINSTON

A Harcourt Education Company

Austin • Orlando • Chicago • New York • Toronto • London • San Diego

Printed in the United States of America

ISBN 0-03-068311-4/0-03-067694-0
3 4 5 6 7 8 9 082 06 05

Contents

Graphic Organizer Activities

TO THE TEACHER

Each chapter of the Student Edition has a graphic organizer activity that focuses on one aspect of chapter content. The graphic organizer activities provide you with a way to help students organize information. The different organizers allow you to meet the varied learning styles of students, and they provide students with an alternative study aid.

Name _____ Class _____ Date _____

We the People

Welcome to America

As a citizen of the United States you have many different reasons to take pride in your country. Imagine that you have been selected to write a letter to a recent immigrant who is thinking of becoming a U.S. citizen. Complete the graphic organizer by supplying the information asked for.

Dear _____,

Explain the role of a citizen of the United States.

_____

_____

_____

_____

Outline the steps an immigrant would need to follow to apply for citizenship.

_____

_____

_____

_____

Describe what you like best about being a citizen of the United States.

_____

_____

_____

_____

Welcome to America

As a citizen of the United States you have many different reasons to take pride in your country. Imagine that you have been selected to write a letter to a recent immigrant who is thinking of becoming a U.S. citizen. Complete the graphic organizer by supplying the information asked for.

Dear _____,

Explain the role of a citizen of the United States.

As a citizen of the United States, you will have the opportunity to vote and work for a political party. You must inform officials in government of your needs or disagreements and know how your government works.

Outline the steps an immigrant would need to follow to apply for citizenship.

All aliens living in the United States must register with the U.S. Immigration and Naturalization Service every year and keep the service informed of their current address. They must be a resident for five years. They must be 18 to apply. They must prove they are free from certain diseases, are not mentally ill, and are not drug addicts or criminals. They must fill out an application called a petition for naturalization. They then meet with an immigration official. They are quizzed about American history and they must prove they can read, write, and speak English. They must believe in the principles of the American government.

Aliens then file their petition for naturalization. They must take an oath of allegiance to the United States in a public ceremony and are granted a certificate of naturalization.

Describe what you like best about being a citizen of the United States.

Students' answers will vary.

Name _____ Class _____ Date _____

CHAPTER **2** Graphic Organizer Activity

Foundations of Government

You and Your Government

To govern means to rule. A government is any organization set up to make and enforce rules. Depending on the government structure, these rules might only benefit a few people in a country at the expense of the many. Other government structures might ensure the greatest good for the greatest number. Complete the graphic organizer by supplying the appropriate information.

Type of Government	Who Benefits?	Why?
Monarchies		
Dictatorships		
Democracies		

You and Your Government

To govern means to rule. A government is any organization set up to make and enforce rules. Depending on the government structure, these rules might only benefit a few people in a country at the expense of the many. Other government structures might ensure the greatest good for the greatest number. Complete the graphic organizer by supplying the appropriate information.

Type of Government	Who Benefits?	Why?
Monarchies	*The royal family and the aristocrats*	*The royal family possesses all the power. It controls the government and most of the laws benefit its members.*
Dictatorships	*The dictators have absolute power. They answer only to themselves, not to the people they govern.*	*Dictators control all aspects of citizens' lives, including their religious, cultural, political, and even personal lives. They hope to gain personally or to enforce their own beliefs.*
Democracies	*The people benefit in a democracy because they rule either directly or through elected officials.*	*By allowing people to make laws and choose rulers, democracies ensure that laws and rulers will benefit the people. Government officials, as public servants, carry out the will of the people.*

Name _____ Class _____ Date _____

Power in the Constitution

The U.S. Constitution outlines three types of powers that governments possess. Complete the graphic organizer by listing examples of each of the powers shown.

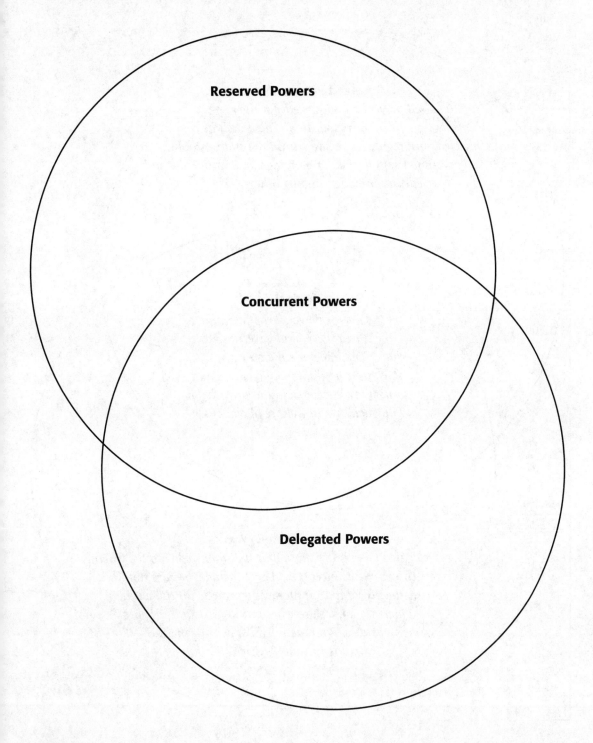

Reserved Powers

Concurrent Powers

Delegated Powers

Power in the Constitution

The U.S. Constitution outlines three types of powers that governments possess. Complete the graphic organizer by listing examples of each of the powers shown.

Reserved Powers

Reserved powers are those kept for the states when the Constitution was written. These include conducting elections, regulating trade within the state, establishing local governments, and making marriage and family law and education policy, among others.

Concurrent Powers

Concurrent powers are those that the state and federal governments share. These include the power to tax, to charter banks, to enforce laws and punish lawbreakers, and to provide for the health and welfare of citizens.

Delegated Powers

Delegated powers are those that the states ceded to the federal government at its inception. These include, but are not limited to, the power to coin money, to provide for the national defense, to declare war, and to raise and support armies. For a detailed list consult the U.S. Constitution, Article I, Section 8.

The Bill of Rights

The U.S. Constitution guarantees U.S. citizens many rights. Many of the rights can be found in the first 10 amendments to the Constitution, also referred to as the Bill of Rights. Complete the graphic organizer by placing a specific right under the amendment in which it is found in the Constitution.

Specific Rights Guaranteed

Speedy and public trial

Freedom of speech

Protection against cruel and unusual punishment

Bail

No quartering of troops

Protection against unreasonable searches and seizures

Guarantees rights not specifically stated

Freedom of assembly

Due process

Powers not delegated to the federal government are reserved to the states or to the people

Bear arms

Protection against self-incrimination

Call witnesses on own behalf

Freedom of religion

Counsel

Freedom of petition

Grand jury review

Be informed of charges against you

Freedom of the press

Protection against double jeopardy

Sue for damages in a civil court

Eminent domain

Amendments

First Amendment	Second Amendment
	Third Amendment
Fourth Amendment	**Fifth Amendment**
Sixth Amendment	**Seventh Amendment**
	Eighth Amendment
Ninth Amendment	**Tenth Amendment**

The Bill of Rights

The U.S. Constitution guarantees U.S. citizens many rights. Many of the rights can be found in the first 10 amendments to the Constitution, also referred to as the Bill of Rights. Complete the graphic organizer by placing a specific right under the amendment in which it is found in the Constitution.

Specific Rights Guaranteed

Speedy and public trial

Freedom of speech

Protection against cruel and unusual punishment

Bail

No quartering of troops

Protection against unreasonable searches and seizures

Guarantees rights not specifically stated

Freedom of assembly

Due process

Powers not delegated to the federal government are reserved to the states or to the people

Bear arms

Protection against self-incrimination

Call witnesses on own behalf

Freedom of religion

Counsel

Freedom of petition

Grand jury review

Be informed of charges against you

Freedom of the press

Protection against double jeopardy

Sue for damages in a civil court

Eminent domain

Amendments

First Amendment	**Second Amendment**
Freedom of assembly *Freedom of the press* *Freedom of religion* *Freedom of speech* *Freedom of petition*	*Bear arms*
	Third Amendment
	No quartering of troops

Fourth Amendment	**Fifth Amendment**
Protection against unreasonable searches and seizures	*Grand jury review* *Due process* *Protection against self-incrimination* *Eminent domain* *Double jeopardy*

Sixth Amendment	**Seventh Amendment**
Speedy and public trial *Counsel* *Call witnesses on own behalf* *Be informed of charges against you*	*Sue for damages in civil court*
	Eighth Amendment
	Protection against cruel and unusual punishment; bail

Ninth Amendment	**Tenth Amendment**
Guarantees rights not specifically listed	*Powers not delegated to the federal government are reserved to states or people*

Graphic Organizer Activity

The Legislative Branch

Know the Congress

Complete the graphic organizer by describing the relationship between the following terms.

census		House of Representatives
apportionment		gerrymandering
members of Congress		franking privilege
House of Representatives		Speaker of the House
floor leader		party whip
U.S. Senate		vice president
bill		law

Know the Congress

Complete the graphic organizer by describing the relationship between the following terms.

census	*Every 10 years, based on the national census, Congress determines how seats in the House of Representatives should be distributed among the states.*	House of Representatives
apportionment	*During the apportionment process state legislators might attempt to draw district boundaries to favor a particular political party, politician, or group of people.*	gerrymandering
members of Congress	*Members of Congress are allowed free mailing privileges for official packages and letters.*	franking privilege
House of Representatives	*Members of the majority party in the House of Representatives choose a leader, known as the Speaker of the House.*	Speaker of the House
floor leader	*The floor leader guides legislation through the debate process, aided by the party whip, whose job it is to see to it that party members vote for party-sponsored legislation.*	party whip
U.S. Senate	*The vice president presides over the U.S. Senate.*	vice president
bill	*A bill is a proposed law. Once Congress has passed the bill and the president has signed it, the bill becomes a law and must be carried out.*	law

 **CHAPTER 6**   Graphic Organizer Activity

The Executive Branch

The President's Many Hats

The President of the United States has many roles and duties. Complete the graphic organizer by describing the many responsibilities of the president.

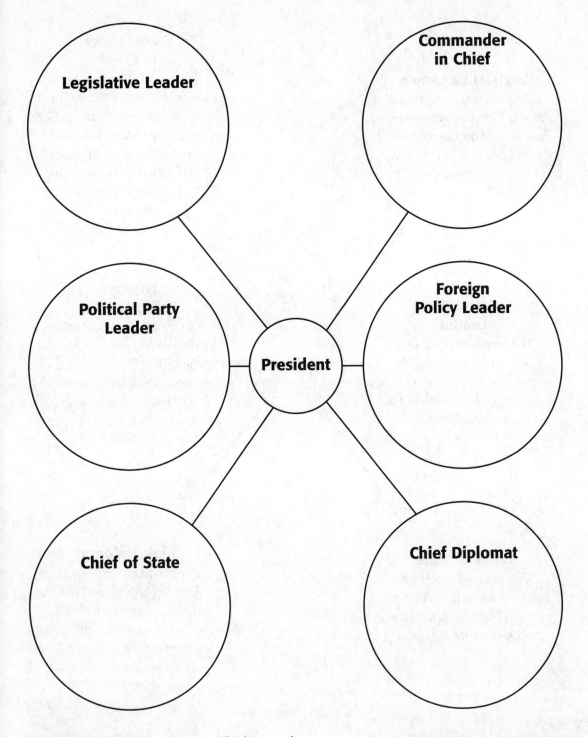

The President's Many Hats

The President of the United States has many roles and duties. Complete the graphic organizer by describing the many responsibilities of the president.

Legislative Leader
The president recommends laws to Congress, recommends how to raise and spend money, and has veto power over legislation.

Commander in Chief
The president is the commander in chief of the military forces of the United States. The Constitution places this power in the hands of the highest-ranking civilian in the country, subject to the will of the voters.

Political Party Leader
The president is the most nationally recognizable member of his party and is the party's spokesperson on the national level.

President

Foreign Policy Leader
The president is responsible for determining the best interest of the United States in terms of its dealings with other nations. The president negotiates treaties with other nations.

Chief of State
The president meets with other world leaders and diplomats. The president is the spokesperson for the country.

Chief Diplomat
The president is the chief diplomat. The president travels to other countries to build international friendships and promote the country's interests.

CHAPTER  7 Graphic Organizer Activity

The Judicial Branch

Landmark Decisions

The Supreme Court has handed down many decisions in its long history. Some of these decisions have had a great impact on the lives of ordinary Americans. These decisions are known as landmark decisions. Complete the graphic organizer with information concerning the landmark cases noted.

Case	Date	Decision	Importance
Marbury v. *Madison*			
Plessy v. *Ferguson*			
Brown v. *Board of Education of Topeka*			
Miranda v. *Arizona*			

Landmark Decisions

The Supreme Court has handed down many decisions in its long history. Some of these decisions have had a great impact on the lives of ordinary Americans. These decisions are known as landmark decisions. Complete the graphic organizer with information concerning the landmark cases noted.

Case	Date	Decision	Importance
Marbury v. *Madison*	1803	*Ruled the Judiciary Act of 1789 unconstitutional*	*This was the first time the Supreme Court exercised the power of judicial review.*
Plessy v. *Ferguson*	1896	*Declared that "separate but equal" facilities on public transportation did not violate the Fourteenth Amendment's guarantee of equal protection.*	*Resulted in legalized (de jure) segregation based on race.*
Brown v. *Board of Education of Topeka*	1954	*Reversed the Plessy decision and declared that "separate but equal" facilities were "inherently unequal."*	*Segregated schools were no longer allowed.*
Miranda v. *Arizona*	1966	*Ruled that a citizen must be informed of his or her rights when being questioned by the police.*	*This ensures that citizens are informed of their rights and as a result their rights will be protected. The "Miranda warnings" are considered parts of due process.*

CHAPTER **8**   Graphic Organizer Activity

Your State Government

Complete the graphic organizer by providing information about your state government in the appropriate areas.

Branches of Government

		Legislative	Executive	Judicial
L E V E L S O F G O V E R N M E N T	**Federal**	Congress—House of Representatives, U.S. Senate	The president and the vice president	The Supreme Court
	State	Describe your state legislature	Name your state's chief executive officer	Outline your state court system

Your State Government

Complete the graphic organizer by providing information about your state government in the appropriate areas.

Branches of Government

		Legislative	Executive	Judicial
L E V E L S O F G O V E R N M E N T	**Federal**	Congress—House of Representatives, U.S. Senate	The president and the vice president	The Supreme Court
	State	Describe your state legislature	Name your state's chief executive officer	Outline your state court system

Student answers will vary depending on their state.

Graphic Organizer Activity

Local Government

How Governments Work Together

Under the federal system in our Constitution, governmental power is divided between levels and branches of government. Complete the graphic organizer by supplying the information called for.

Branches of Government

	Executive	Legislative	Judicial
Federal			
State			
Local			

Levels of Government

How Governments Work Together

Under the federal system in our Constitution, governmental power is divided between levels and branches of government. Complete the graphic organizer by supplying the information called for.

Branches of Government

Levels of Government		Executive	Legislative	Judicial
	Federal	*president* *vice president*	*The Congress* *U.S. Senate* *U.S. House of Representatives*	*U.S. Supreme Court* *U.S. Courts of Appeals* *Federal District Courts*
	State	*The information here should reflect the appropriate titles for your state.*		
	Local	*The information here should reflect the appropriate titles for your locality.*		

Name _____ Class _____ Date _____

Politics and the Vote

Complete the graphic organizer by explaining the relationship between the following terms.

political party ⟨   ⟩ candidate

Democratic Party ⟨   ⟩ Republican Party

political party ⟨   ⟩ national committee

voters ⟨   ⟩ polling place

registration ⟨   ⟩ voting

primary election ⟨   ⟩ general election

candidate ⟨   ⟩ party platform

election of the president ⟨   ⟩ electoral college

Politics and the Vote

Complete the graphic organizer by explaining the relationship between the following terms.

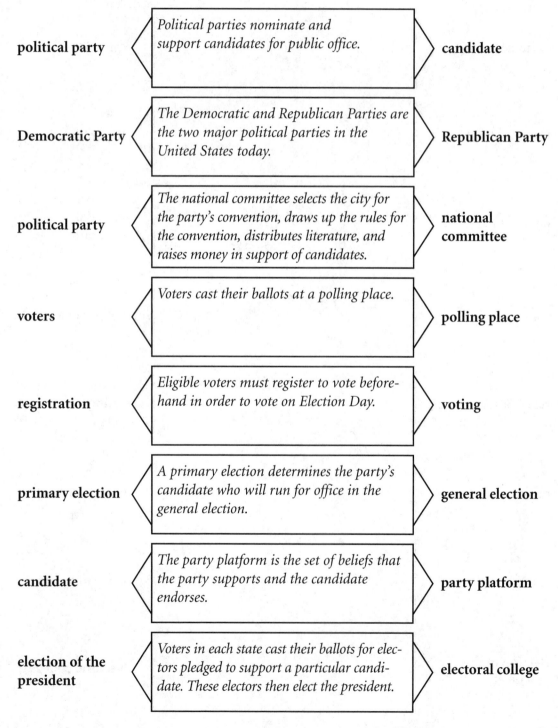

political party — *Political parties nominate and support candidates for public office.* — **candidate**

Democratic Party — *The Democratic and Republican Parties are the two major political parties in the United States today.* — **Republican Party**

political party — *The national committee selects the city for the party's convention, draws up the rules for the convention, distributes literature, and raises money in support of candidates.* — **national committee**

voters — *Voters cast their ballots at a polling place.* — **polling place**

registration — *Eligible voters must register to vote beforehand in order to vote on Election Day.* — **voting**

primary election — *A primary election determines the party's candidate who will run for office in the general election.* — **general election**

candidate — *The party platform is the set of beliefs that the party supports and the candidate endorses.* — **party platform**

election of the president — *Voters in each state cast their ballots for electors pledged to support a particular candidate. These electors then elect the president.* — **electoral college**

The American Political System

The American political system is influenced by a variety of factors. Complete the graphic organizer by describing each of the terms listed.

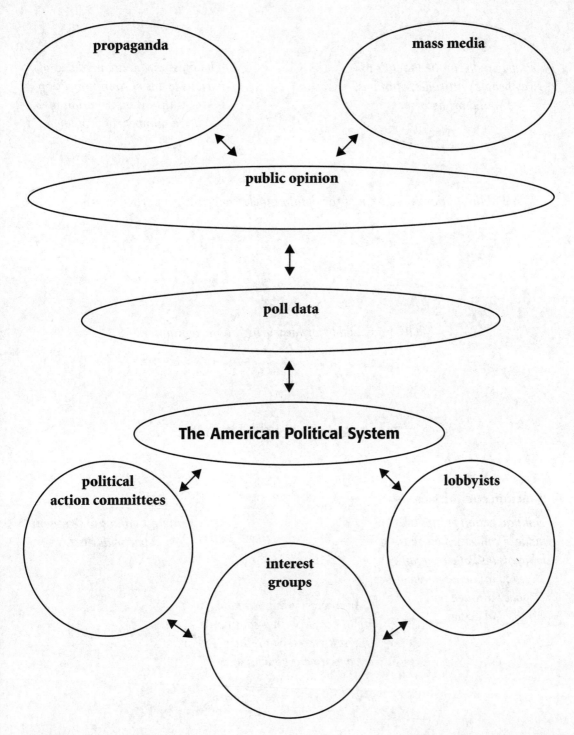

The American Political System

The American political system is influenced by a variety of factors. Complete the graphic organizer by describing each of the terms listed.

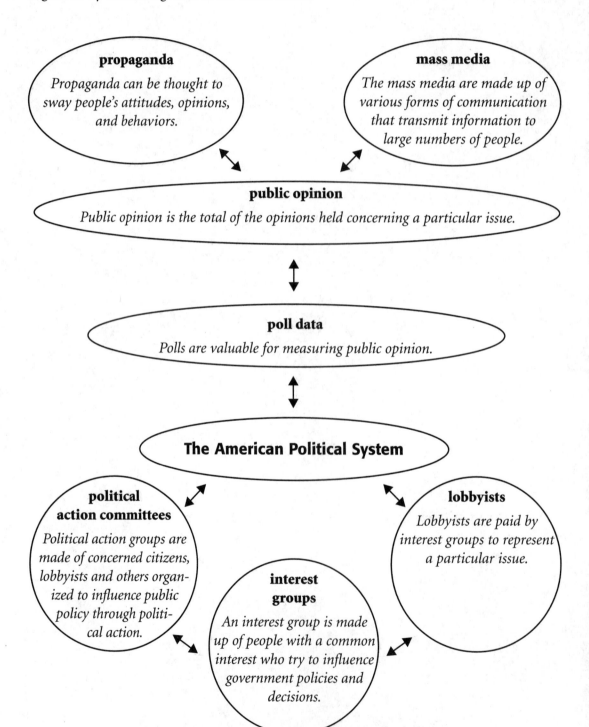

CHAPTER 12

Graphic Organizer Activity

Paying for Government

Types of Taxes

The costs of government are paid with public funds. Much of this funding is raised by taxes. Complete the graphic organizer by explaining the various types of taxes employed by the government.

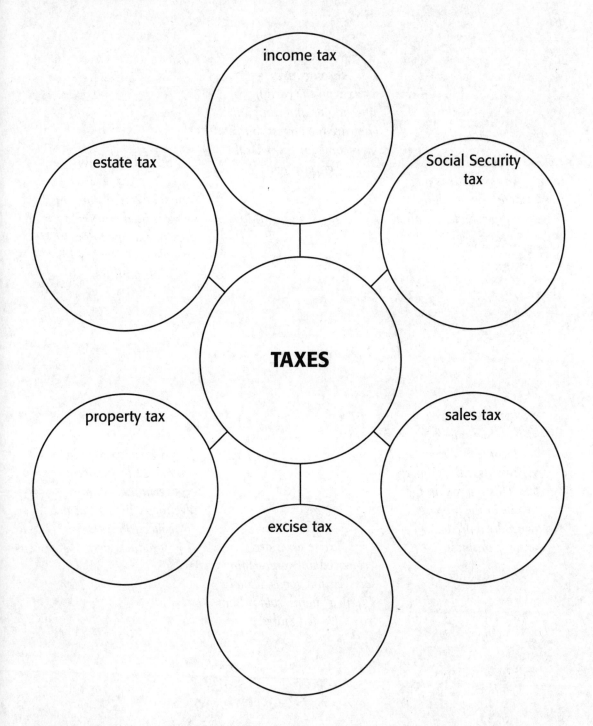

Types of Taxes

The costs of government are paid with public funds. Much of this funding is raised by taxes. Complete the graphic organizer by explaining the various types of taxes employed by the government.

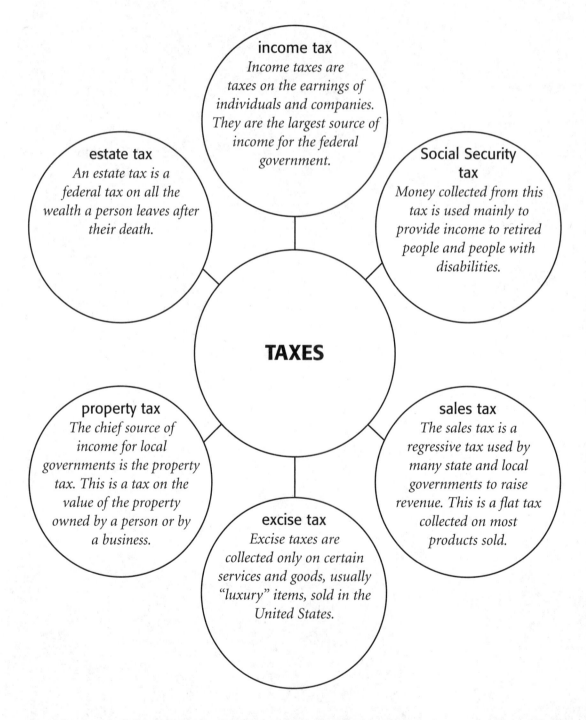

income tax
Income taxes are taxes on the earnings of individuals and companies. They are the largest source of income for the federal government.

estate tax
An estate tax is a federal tax on all the wealth a person leaves after their death.

Social Security tax
Money collected from this tax is used mainly to provide income to retired people and people with disabilities.

TAXES

property tax
The chief source of income for local governments is the property tax. This is a tax on the value of the property owned by a person or by a business.

sales tax
The sales tax is a regressive tax used by many state and local governments to raise revenue. This is a flat tax collected on most products sold.

excise tax
Excise taxes are collected only on certain services and goods, usually "luxury" items, sold in the United States.

CHAPTER 13

Graphic Organizer Activity

Citizenship and the Family

The Modern American Family

The American family can be influenced by a number of factors. Complete the graphic organizer by describing how the factors shown can influence a family.

Challenge
Research Stats
marriage laws

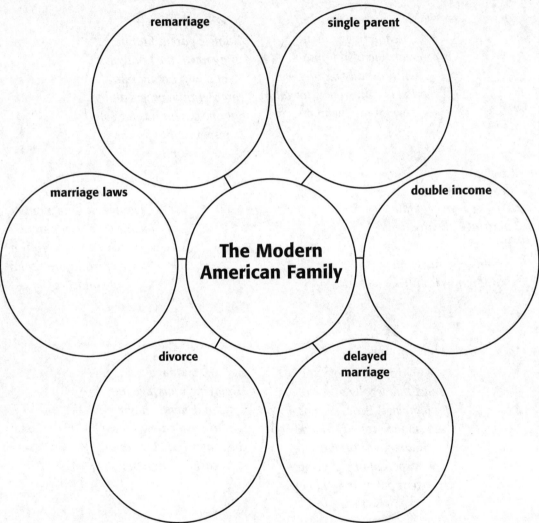

The Modern American Family

The American family can be influenced by a number of factors. Complete the graphic organizer by describing how the factors shown can influence a family.

remarriage
Remarriages often create blended families, which usually require a period of adjustment for all new family members.

single parent
Single parent families may mean the family is in a lower economic bracket than others and that one parent has the sole responsibility for the family.

marriage laws
These laws regulate marriage, divorce, and the responsibilities and rights of adults and children in families.

The Modern American Family

double income
Double income often means that both parents work, which may result in change of traditional roles of childcare.

divorce
Divorce is an official act that legally dissolves a marriage. Issues such as a division of property, custody of children, visitation rights, and spousal and child support payments will be settled.

delayed marriage
Delaying marriage may mean delaying having children so parents may be somewhat older than earlier families.

Name _____ Class _____ Date _____

Citizenship in School

Education and You

Complete the graphic organizer with information about education in the United States.

What are the values that have guided American education?

What is the relationship between good study skills and doing well on tests?

What is the motivation for learning?

What is the relationship between critical thinking and problem solving?

Citizenship in School

Education and You

Complete the graphic organizer with information about education in the United States.

What are the values that have guided American education?

American education is based on the beliefs that (1) all citizens should receive free education, (2) no one should be discriminated against, (3) religion should not be part of public education, (4) local school districts have day-to-day control, (5) states should require children to attend school or be homeschooled, and (6) states should provide an enriching environment.

What is the relationship between good study skills and doing well on tests?

Tests require concentration and care. Keeping up with class work and assignments by using proper study skills can improve performance on tests.

What is the motivation for learning?

Motivation is the internal drive that stirs people and directs their attitudes and behavior. Motivated people are curious about how the world works and therefore seek information.

What is the relationship between critical thinking and problem solving?

Critical thinking involves several steps. This type of reasoning is made of defining the problem at hand, distinguishing fact from opinion, weighing the evidence, and reaching a conclusion. It is important to keep an open mind so the solution you envision is not influenced by prejudice.

Name _____ Class _____ Date _____

Doing Your Part

As a member of a community you have an obligation to be a positive influence on that community. Complete the graphic organizer by writing a letter describing a project that you think would improve the lives of the people in your community. Address your letter to the appropriate community official.

Dear _____ ,

                                                        Sincerely,

Doing Your Part

As a member of a community you have an obligation to be a positive influence on that community. Complete the graphic organizer by writing a letter describing a project that you think would improve the lives of the people in your community. Address your letter to the appropriate community official.

Dear _____ ,

Student responses will vary.

Sincerely,

Name _____ Class _____ Date _____

CHAPTER 16

Graphic Organizer Activity

Citizenship and the Law

Causes of Crime

Although no one knows what motivates a person to commit a crime, many theories exist as to its cause. For each theory of crime, write the cause in the box on the left and the possible effect in the box on the right.

Cause	Theory	Effect
	poverty →	
	illegal drug use →	
	urbanization →	
	permissiveness →	

In your opinion, which theory best explains what motivates a person in a criminal activity?

Can you suggest a solution?

Citizenship and the Law

Causes of Crime

Although no one knows what motivates a person to commit a crime, many theories exist as to its cause. For each theory of crime, write the cause in the box on the left and the possible effect in the box on the right.

Cause	Theory	Effect
Many undereducated people live in overcrowded, rundown areas, and earn below the poverty level.	**poverty** →	*As a result, some may feel helpless and angry and may turn to breaking the law to try to obtain things they do not have.*
Many mind-altering substances are illegal. People addicted to these substances break the law to get them.	**illegal drug use** →	*People addicted to drugs sometimes break the law to support an expensive habit. Often their judgment is clouded and they make inappropriate decisions, which leads them into trouble with the law.*
High population density exists in cities. This provides more opportunity for criminal activity.	**urbanization** →	*Large numbers of young people live in cities, and they account for half of all those arrested in the United States.*
This theory holds that children are spoiled, and they are permitted by their parents to do what they want.	**permissiveness** →	*As a result, they cannot control their behavior and find it difficult to conform to the rules of law.*

In your opinion, which theory best explains what motivates a person in a criminal activity?

Student answers will vary.

Can you suggest a solution?

Student answers will vary.

CHAPTER 17 Graphic Organizer Activity

The Economic System

The Economic System at Work

Complete the graphic organizer by describing the relationship between the following pairs of economic terms.

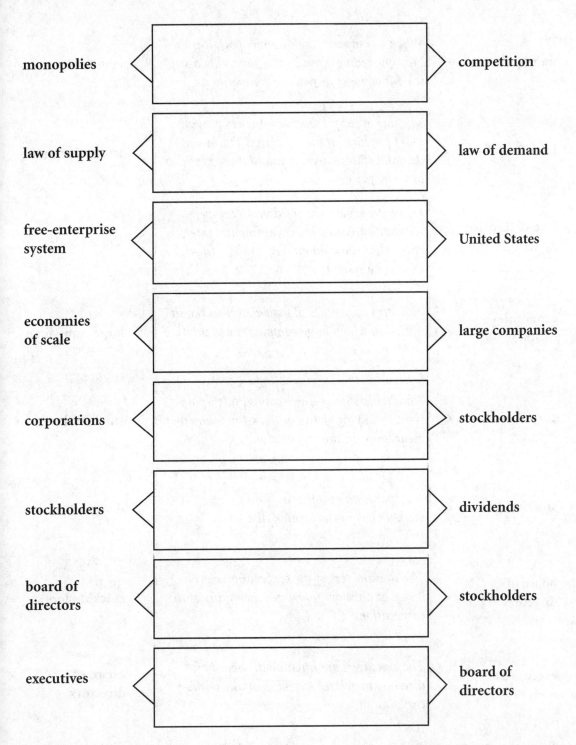

monopolies ◁ ▷ competition

law of supply ◁ ▷ law of demand

free-enterprise system ◁ ▷ United States

economies of scale ◁ ▷ large companies

corporations ◁ ▷ stockholders

stockholders ◁ ▷ dividends

board of directors ◁ ▷ stockholders

executives ◁ ▷ board of directors

The Economic System at Work

Complete the graphic organizer by describing the relationship between the following pairs of economic terms.

| monopolies | When a company holds a monopoly, it is the only one selling a product or supplying a service. Monopolies drown out competition. | competition |

| law of supply | The law of supply states businesses provide more products at higher prices. The law of demand states buyers demand more products at lower prices. | law of demand |

| free-enterprise system | Free enterprise is the freedom to compete without unreasonable governmental interference. The U.S. economic system is a free-enterprise system. | United States |

| economies of scale | The term economies of scale describes the situation in which large companies can produce goods more efficiently. | large companies |

| corporations | Stockholders invest their capital in corporations by buying shares of stock (or shares of ownership) in the corporation. | stockholders |

| stockholders | A corporation's profits are paid to stockholders in the form of dividends. | dividends |

| board of directors | The stockholders of the corporation elect a board of directors to oversee the affairs of the corporation. | stockholders |

| executives | The executives are hired by the board of directors to oversee the daily affairs of the corporation. | board of directors |

Name _____ Class _____ Date _____

 Graphic Organizer Activity

Goods and Services

From Factory to you

The United States economic system has an extraordinary ability to produce goods and services. Complete the graphic organizer by explaining what part each element plays in the economic system of the United States.

Mass Production   **System of Distribution**   **Consumer**

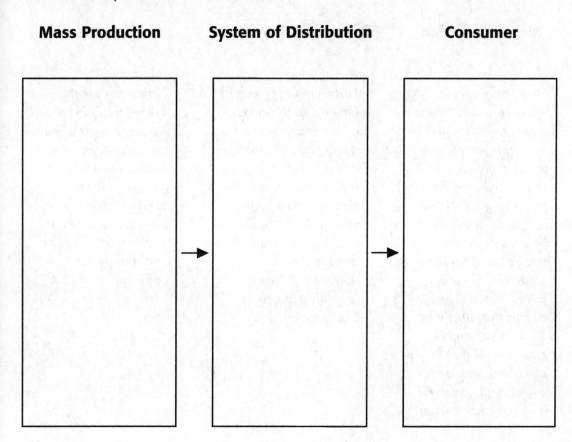

Create an advertisement for either a real or imaginary product that you think would be of benefit to people your age.

Goods and Services

From Factory to you

The United States economic system has an extraordinary ability to produce goods and services. Complete the graphic organizer by explaining what part each element plays in the economic system of the United States.

Mass Production	**System of Distribution**	**Consumer**
Mass production by machines allows for the rapid production of large numbers of identical objects, thereby reducing the price charged for these objects. Although mass production techniques involve the use of many machines, they also require human labor, thereby providing jobs. Urban areas tend to grow around the manufacturing centers providing employment for a host of other workers.	Distribution of goods is essential to the success of any enterprise. Airplanes, railroads, and an effective highway system are key elements. Such routes crisscross our nation. Entire industries have developed in the movement of goods from one place to another.	Consumers are the driving forces in the economic system. They create the demand for products and services and spend the money to acquire them. They also provide the brains and/or labor to create and transport the products.

Create an advertisement for either a real or imaginary product that you think would be of benefit to people your age.

Student answers will vary.

CHAPTER 19   Graphic Organizer Activity
Managing Money

Understanding Currency

Every country of the world has a currency. Complete the graphic organizer by explaining the four common features of all currency.

```
┌─────────────────────┐     ┌─────────────────────┐
│                     │     │                     │
│                     │     │                     │
│                     │     │                     │
│                     │     │                     │
└─────────────────────┘     └─────────────────────┘
            ┌───────────────────────────┐
            │         Currency          │
            └───────────────────────────┘
┌─────────────────────┐     ┌─────────────────────┐
│                     │     │                     │
│                     │     │                     │
│                     │     │                     │
│                     │     │                     │
└─────────────────────┘     └─────────────────────┘


┌─────────────────────┐     ┌─────────────────────┐
│                     │     │                     │
│                     │     │                     │
│                     │     │                     │
│                     │     │                     │
└─────────────────────┘     └─────────────────────┘
         ┌───────────────────────────────┐
         │  How does the currency of the │
         │  United States fit these      │
         │  criteria?                    │
         └───────────────────────────────┘
┌─────────────────────┐     ┌─────────────────────┐
│                     │     │                     │
│                     │     │                     │
│                     │     │                     │
│                     │     │                     │
└─────────────────────┘     └─────────────────────┘
```

Understanding Currency

Every country of the world has a currency. Complete the graphic organizer by explaining the four common features of all currency.

Currency must be easy to carry and take up little space so people can carry it with them for everyday use.	*Currency must be based on a system of units that are easy to multiply and divide. Figuring the number of coins and bills needed to exchange for an item should be easy to do.*

Currency

Currency must be made in a standard form and guaranteed by the government of the country that issues it. In this way citizens can be certain that their coins and bills will be accepted in exchange for goods and services.	*Currency must be durable, or last a long time. It should not wear out too quickly or fall apart. People must be able to keep currency until they are ready to spend it.*

All U.S. bills are of uniform size and color and weigh very little. Coins are lightweight.	*U.S. currency is based on units of ten.*

How does the currency of the United States fit these criteria?

U.S. currency is made by government facilities (called mints) and is stamped with the words "United States of America." The bills have the great seal of the United States as well as the signatures of governmental officials. They also are stamped "legal tender."	*U.S. coins are made of very durable metals and are in circulation for a long time. U.S. bills are made of special paper that is quite durable for the use that each bill gets.*

Graphic Organizer Activity
Economic Challenges

The Business Cycle

The performance of the American economy changes over time. This is called the business cycle. Complete the graphic organizer by describing the elements of the business cycle.

Contraction

Peak

Recession

Expansion

Trough

The Business Cycle

The performance of the American economy changes over time. This is called the business cycle. Complete the graphic organizer by describing the elements of the business cycle.

Contraction

The economy slows down, and demand for goods and services lessens.

Peak

Business is good, jobs are plentiful, and profits are high.

Recession

Businesses fail, profits fall, unemployment rises.

Expansion

The economy grows, employment grows, and demand for goods and services increases.

Trough

Depression; period of less demand for goods and services and high unemployment

Name _____ Class _____ Date _____

Economic Systems of the World

There are many different economic systems in the world today. Complete the graphic organizer by describing the three basic economic systems on which the others are based.

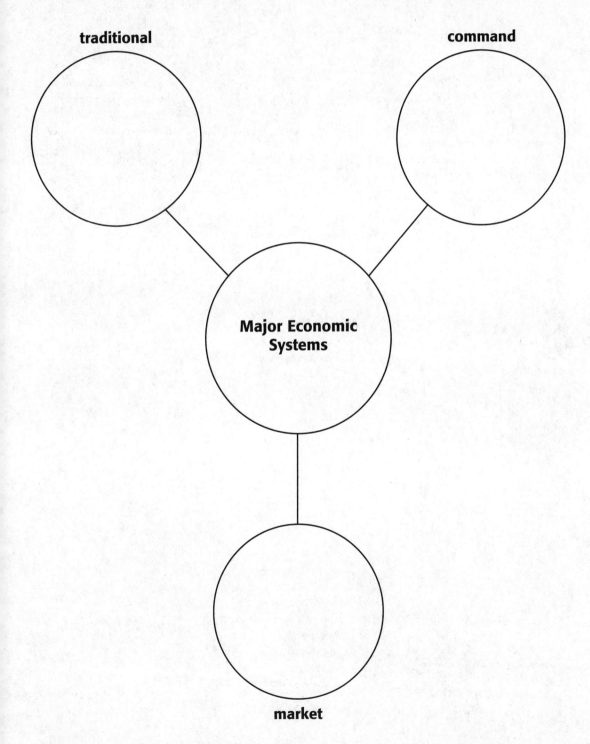

traditional

command

Major Economic Systems

market

The U.S. Economy and the World

Economic Systems of the World

There are many different economic systems in the world today. Complete the graphic organizer by describing the three basic economic systems on which the others are based.

traditional

This type of economy is based on customs and traditions. Generally goods and services are distributed among all members of the society. Many of these economies are dependent on hunting and gathering, and the fruits of labor are shared.

command

Government officials make economic plans for the country. They decide how resources will be allocated and which goods will be made and how. This type of economy often was present in communist countries.

Major Economic Systems

Government plays a limited role in making economic decisions. Goods and services are exchanged with limited government interference in this economic system.

market

Name _____ Class _____ Date _____

Learning about Careers

Imagine that you have already embarked on a career and have been asked to give a talk and explain why you chose the career you did. Complete the graphic organizer below to help you organize your thoughts.

Title: Why I have chosen the career of _____.

Explain the kind of work you do.

What personal qualities does the job require?

How much education or training did the job require?

How many job opportunities exist in this field?

What is your approximate salary?

How do you feel about this job or career choice?

Where do you have to live in order to do this job?

Learning about Careers

Imagine that you have already embarked on a career and have been asked to give a talk and explain why you chose the career you did. Complete the graphic organizer below to help you organize your thoughts.

Title: Why I have chosen the career of _____.

Explain the kind of work you do.

> *Student answers will vary depending on the job/career choices they have made.*

What personal qualities does the job require?

> *Student answers will vary depending on the job/career choices they have made.*

How much education or training did the job require?

> *Student answers will vary depending on the job/career choices they have made.*

How many job opportunities exist in this field?

> *Student answers will vary depending on the job/career choices they have made.*

What is your approximate salary?

> *Student answers will vary depending on the job/career choices they have made.*

How do you feel about this job or career choice?

> *Student answers will vary depending on the job/career choices they have made.*

Where do you have to live in order to do this job?

> *Student answers will vary depending on the job/career choices they have made.*

Name _____ Class _____ Date _____

Conducting Foreign Relations

The U.S. Constitution has provided for a system of checks and balances among the three branches of the federal government. In the area of foreign policy, the executive and legislative branches exercise the most control. The president often takes the lead in developing and implementing foreign policy. However, congressional power can balance the president's power. Complete the graphic organizer that explains this balancing act.

President   **Congress**

commander in chief
_____
treaty making
_____
names the secretary of state
_____
names ambassadors
_____
determines foreign policy
_____
recommends defense policy
_____

Conducting Foreign Relations

The U.S. Constitution has provided for a system of checks and balances among the three branches of the federal government. In the area of foreign policy, the executive and legislative branches exercise the most control. The president often takes the lead in developing and implementing foreign policy. However, congressional power can balance the president's power. Complete the graphic organizer that explains this balancing act.

President **Congress**

President	Congress
commander in chief	*War Powers Act limits the commander in chief's ability to deploy soldiers. Only Congress can declare war.*
treaty making	*All treaties must be ratified (approved) by the Senate.*
names the secretary of state	*Candidate must be confirmed (approved) by the Senate.*
names ambassadors	*Candidates must be confirmed by the Senate.*
determines foreign policy	*Senate Foreign Relations Committee and the full Senate offer advice and ultimately provide consent.*
recommends defense policy	*Budget is approved by Congress.*

 **CHAPTER 24**

Graphic Organizer Activity

Charting a Course

Developing Foreign Policy

Foreign policy is a country's plan for establishing and maintaining relationships with other nations. Complete the graphic organizer by describing each of the building blocks of American foreign policy.

Development of American Foreign Policy

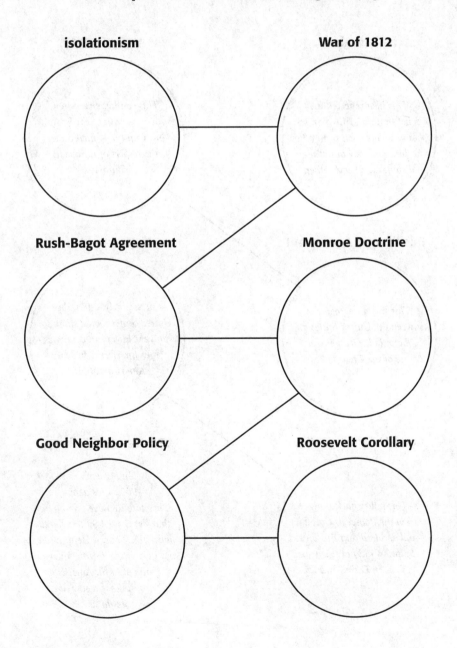

isolationism

War of 1812

Rush-Bagot Agreement

Monroe Doctrine

Good Neighbor Policy

Roosevelt Corollary

CHAPTER 24

Graphic Organizer Activity

Charting a Course

Developing Foreign Policy

Foreign policy is a country's plan for establishing and maintaining relationships with other nations. Complete the graphic organizer by describing each of the building blocks of American foreign policy.

Development of American Foreign Policy

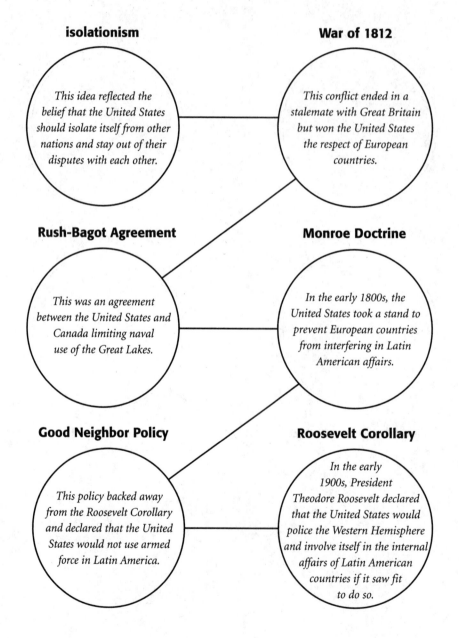

isolationism

This idea reflected the belief that the United States should isolate itself from other nations and stay out of their disputes with each other.

War of 1812

This conflict ended in a stalemate with Great Britain but won the United States the respect of European countries.

Rush-Bagot Agreement

This was an agreement between the United States and Canada limiting naval use of the Great Lakes.

Monroe Doctrine

In the early 1800s, the United States took a stand to prevent European countries from interfering in Latin American affairs.

Good Neighbor Policy

This policy backed away from the Roosevelt Corollary and declared that the United States would not use armed force in Latin America.

Roosevelt Corollary

In the early 1900s, President Theodore Roosevelt declared that the United States would police the Western Hemisphere and involve itself in the internal affairs of Latin American countries if it saw fit to do so.

Name _____ Class _____ Date _____

Improving Life for All Americans

Urban Growth

America began as a rural country with small, scattered settlements. Some small communities grew into cities, and according to the 1920 U.S. Census, more Americans lived in cities than in rural areas. Cities continue to evolve. Complete the graphic organizer by describing the components of an urban area and explaining the impact that transportation, urban decay, and growth has on each component.

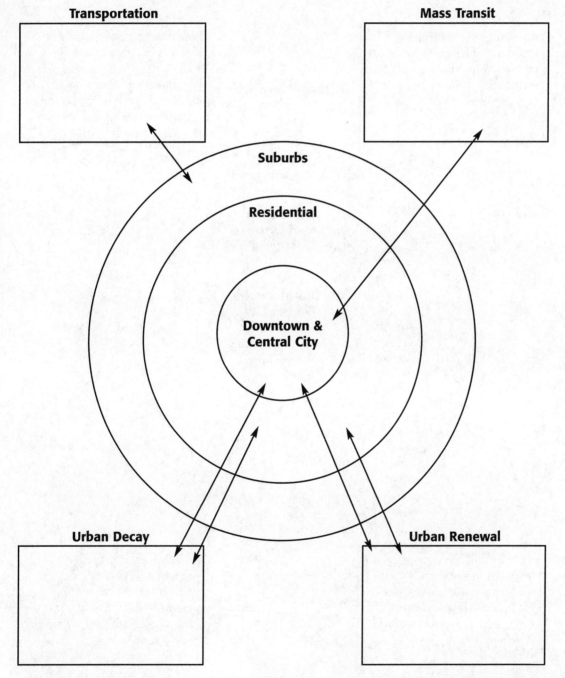

Transportation

Mass Transit

Suburbs

Residential

Downtown & Central City

Urban Decay

Urban Renewal

Improving Life for All Americans

Urban Growth

America began as a rural country with small, scattered settlements. Some small communities grew into cities, and according to the 1920 U.S. Census, more Americans lived in cities than in rural areas. Cities continue to evolve. Complete the graphic organizer by describing the components of an urban area and explaining the impact that transportation, urban decay, and growth has on each component.

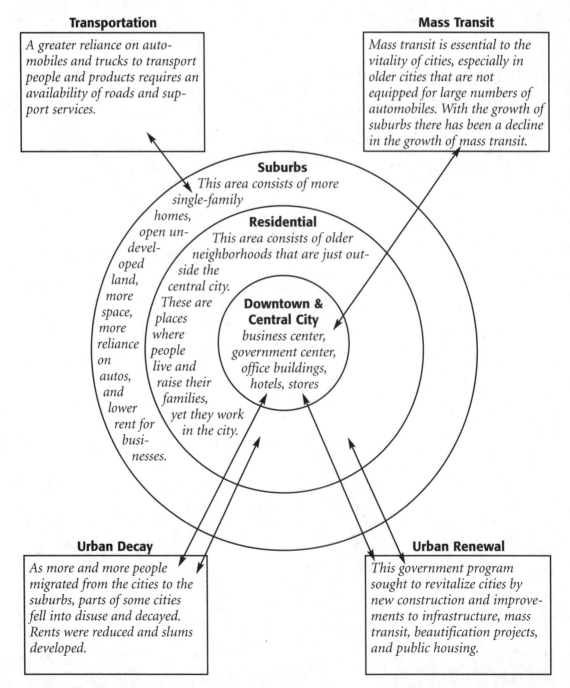

Transportation

A greater reliance on automobiles and trucks to transport people and products requires an availability of roads and support services.

Mass Transit

Mass transit is essential to the vitality of cities, especially in older cities that are not equipped for large numbers of automobiles. With the growth of suburbs there has been a decline in the growth of mass transit.

Suburbs

This area consists of more single-family homes, open undeveloped land, more space, more reliance on autos, and lower rent for businesses.

Residential

This area consists of older neighborhoods that are just outside the central city. These are places where people live and raise their families, yet they work in the city.

Downtown & Central City

business center, government center, office buildings, hotels, stores

Urban Decay

As more and more people migrated from the cities to the suburbs, parts of some cities fell into disuse and decayed. Rents were reduced and slums developed.

Urban Renewal

This government program sought to revitalize cities by new construction and improvements to infrastructure, mass transit, beautification projects, and public housing.

Graphic Organizer Activity

The Global Environment

Our Future on Earth

Congress has passed several laws designed to protect the environment. However, it takes each of us to do our part to keep the Earth healthy. Complete the graphic organizer by explaining each piece of federal legislation listed, as well as connecting those laws to your community.

National Environmental Policy Act
What is your community doing to protect the environment?

Clean Air Acts
Are there any sources of air pollution in your community?

Resource Conservation and Recovery Act
What are the designated routes in your community that allow for the transport of hazardous waste?

Wild and Scenic Rivers Act and Wilderness Act
Are there any areas in your community that are protected by this act or that you think should be?

Endangered Species Acts
Are there any endangered species that live in or migrate through your area?

Our Future on Earth

Congress has passed several laws designed to protect the environment. However, it takes each of us to do our part to keep the Earth healthy. Complete the graphic organizer by explaining each piece of federal legislation listed, as well as connecting those laws to your community.

National Environmental Policy Act

Passed in 1969, this act oversees the country's pollution controls. Student answers on examples from their community will vary.

What is your community doing to protect the environment?

Clean Air Acts

Provide funds for research and set standards for air pollution controls. Student answers on examples from their community will vary.

Are there any sources of air pollution in your community?

Resource Conservation and Recovery Act

Enables the government to regulate the transportation and storage of dangerous chemicals. Student answers on examples from their community will vary.

What are the designated routes in your community that allow for the transport of hazardous waste?

Wild and Scenic Rivers Act and Wilderness Act

Designated areas of land to be kept in their natural state. Student answers on examples from their community will vary.

Are there any areas in your community that are protected by this act or that you think should be?

Endangered Species Acts

Hundreds of plant and animal species are protected from harm by these acts. Student answers on examples from their community will vary.

Are there any endangered species that live in or migrate through your area?
